MAC~~HINE~~ ~~TO~~P

RE~~CO~~RD
BR~~EAKE~~RS

Dani~~el~~ ~~Coombs~~ Pang

This edition published in 2013 by Wayland

Wayland
Hachette Children's Books
338 Euston Road
London NW1 3BH

Wayland Australia
Level 17/207 Kent Street
Sydney, NSW 2000

Produced by
David West Children's Books
7 Princeton Court
55 Felsham Road
London SW15 1AZ

Designer: Rob Shone
Illustrator: Alex Pang
Editor: Katharine Pethick
Consultant: Steve Parker

A CIP catalogue record for this book is available from the British Library.

ISBN: 9780750280259

2 4 6 8 10 9 7 5 3 1

Printed in China

Wayland is a division of
Hachette Children's Books,
an Hachette UK company.
www.hachette.co.uk

PHOTO CREDITS :
Abbreviations: t-top, m-middle, b-bottom, r-right, l-left, c-centre.
4-5, Castrol; 6tr, Andreas Praefcke; 6bl, Castrol, 6br, Alfred John West; 7ml, 7bl, 7br, Castrol; 8t, US Air Force; 8ml, NASA; 8mr, Przemyslaw Jahr; 8b, Joe Mabel; 9t, NASA; 9m, DAMASA; 9bl, Jorfer; 9br, Castrol; 30t, Arpingstone; 30ml, NASA; 30mr, Andreas Manuel Rodriguez; 30b, Martin Roll

CONTENTS

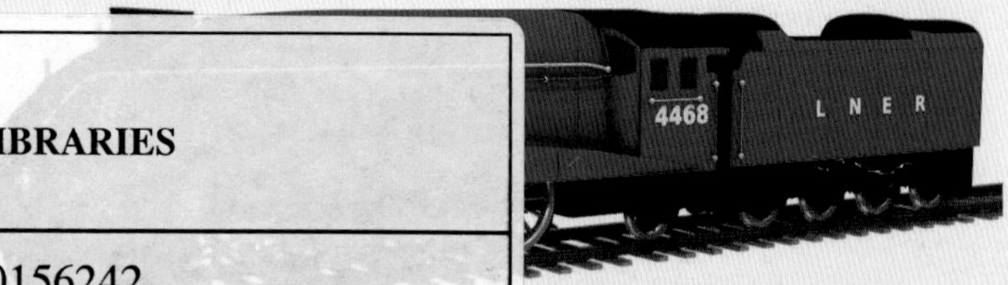

INTRODUCTION

Some people like to take their machines to the limit – drive them hard to see exactly what they can do. But there is a rarer breed who see no limits and want to push the boundaries further. They are the people who design and build record breaking machines.

HOW THIS BOOK WORKS

MAIN TEXT
Gives details of the vehicle's history and explains which record it currently holds. Other information, such as when the record was set, is also covered here.

SPECS
This panel gives information about the vehicle's speed and dimensions.

CLOSE-UP VIEW
Smaller illustrations look in detail at other interesting features, or vehicles or equipment associated with the record breaker when it is in use.

TGV 4402
TGV 4402 is the fastest train ever to run on conventional rails. On 3 April 2007, it set a new world record speed of 574.8 kilometres per hour. TGV 4402 is a one-off train that was specially modified to make the world record attempt. It is based on the TGV POS, which routinely carries passengers through the France at up to 320 kilometres per hour.

TGV 4402
Length: 106 metres
Weight: 268 tonnes
Wheel diameter: 1.092 metres
Top speed: 574.8 kilometres per hour

BRAKES
TGV 4402 has disk brakes on its wheels and dynamic brakes on its axles. Together, these provide enough braking power to stop the train.

PANTOGRAPH
This is used to collect electric current from overhead lines to drive the train. Pantographs are commonly used by trains in France.

TRACK
Unlike the train, LGV Est, where the speed record was achieved, was not modified in any way. It is a standard high-speed train line.

DRIVER'S CAB
The cab of TGV 4402 has a comfortable, soft seat for the driver, surrounded by controls.

Cooling tanks

Pneumatic block

Upper deck

Lower deck

TRANSFORMERS
These convert the electrical power gathered by the pantograph to a voltage the train's engines can use.

POWER PACK
This receives electricity from the transformers and uses it to drive the wheels of the locomotive.

MOTOR BOGIE
Each of TGV 4402's two locomotives sits on two of these. For the record attempt two were added to one of the carriages. Despite their name, TGV motor bogies do not have their own motors – instead they use a system of gears to transfer power from the power pack to the wheels.

DUPLEX CARRIAGES
Three of these double-decker carriages were used between two TGV locomotives to make up the record-breaking train.

Permanent-magnet motor

Secondary suspension

Primary suspension

MAIN ILLUSTRATION
This exploded illustration shows the internal structure of the vehicle and gives information on the positions of its various working parts.

INTERESTING FEATURES
This box contains a detailed illustration of the engine or other design features that make the vehicle unique. Informative text explains the feature's function.

PAST RECORDS

Records come and records go. Most of the record breaking vehicles of today are just the latest in a long line of title holders.

WRIGHT FLYER III
In 1905, this early plane took the air speed record after travelling at 56 km/h.

BENZ MOTORWAGEN
The first true motor car, this held the first motor car speed record, a staggeringly slow 13 km/h.

FIRST MOTOR VEHICLES

Theoretically, the land speed record for wheeled vehicles can be traced back to the chariots of Rome. However, most authorities begin their lists with motor cars. The earliest motor car, the Benz Motorwagen, was built in 1885. Today's record holder is almost 100 times faster.

WATER AND AIR

Before the invention of the steam engine, water speed records were held and broken by sailing vessels. Air speed records began with the first powered flight, around the start of the 20th century. For years, aeroplanes remained slower than boats.

TURBINIA
In 1897, this steamship reached 62.9 km/h, breaking the water speed record.

WAKEFIELD TROPHY
Commissioned in 1928, this was awarded to early holders of the land speed record.

BUILT FOR SPEED

When the first motor cars were built speed was not really a consideration. It was more than a decade before cars were really tested to see how fast they could go. However, once cars started moving really quickly the bug soon caught on. Even so, it would be the 1920s before cars could move faster than trains.

GIANT SHIPS

Not all records are about speed – size is important too. This was demonstrated by the excitement surrounding the launch of the Titanic. In 1911, her statistics were listed in newspapers all over the world.

RMS TITANIC
Weighing 53,146 tonnes, this ship was the world's largest before she sank in 1912.

ELECTRICITY AND STEAM
In 1899, the electric La Jamais Contente (top) became the first vehicle to reach 100 km/h. The steam-driven Stanley Rocket Racer (below) passed the 200 km/h mark in 1906.

MISS ENGLAND II
In 1930, this British boat took the water speed record to 158.94 km/h.

SUPERMARINE SEAPLANES
These were the fastest vehicles on Earth in 1931, with one reaching 655.8 km/h.

SUNBEAM
In 1927, this car became the first to exceed 322 km/h, driven by Henry Segrave.

THE MODERN AGE

During the 20th century, motor vehicles and aircraft increasingly became part of our lives. As their numbers grew, their design evolved – becoming quicker and more efficient than before.

ME 262
This German jet took the air speed record in 1944, reaching 1,004 km/h.

THE JET AGE

War provided the stimulus for ever faster aircraft. During World War II, German engineers developed the first jet engines. These took planes to speeds never dreamt of before.

BELL X-1
In 1947 this became the first manned vehicle to travel faster than the speed of sound.

BLUEBIRD CN7
In 1964, this Bluebird took the record for a four-wheeled car to 648.73 km/h.

STREAMLINING

By the late 1920s, teams from both sides of the Atlantic were battling for the land speed record. Along with power, streamlining became an important feature. The transatlantic fight also spread on to the water, with speed titles swapping hands every few years.

SLO-MO-SHUN IV
Piloted by the American Stan Sayres, this propeller-driven boat took the water speed record up to 287.2 km/h in 1952.

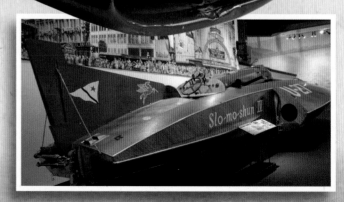

MILITARY MUSCLE

While the fastest cars and boats are built by civilians, the fastest aircraft have long been built for military use. Part of the reason for this is the massive cost involved in developing new aircraft. The SR-71 Blackbird programme, for example, cost more than US$1 billion.

ENDURANCE TESTS

Many modern records celebrate fuel economy and endurance rather than speed. One example of this is the battle to be fastest to fly around the globe without refuelling.

SR-71 BLACKBIRD
This US military aircraft holds the speed record for manned aircraft, at 3,530 km/h.

SHINKANSEN BULLET TRAINS
These Japanese trains set world record rail speeds in the 1960s and 1970s and are still in use.

VOYAGER
In 1986, this aircraft, piloted by the American Dick Rutan, became the first to fly around the world without refuelling.

THRUST 2
This car held the world land speed record from 1983 to 1997. Its driver, Richard Noble, developed the current holder, Thrust SSC.

LNER CLASS A4 MALLARD

Mallard was the fastest steam locomotive ever built. It set its record speed of 203 kilometres per hour in 1938. At that time Mallard was just five months old. Having remained in service with the London and North Eastern Railway (LNER) until 1963, it was restored to working order in the 1980s. It is now in the National Railway Museum in York.

STREAMLINED BODYWORK

Mallard's smooth shape helped increase its speed. It also enabled smoke from the chimney to be blown away from the driver's cab.

LNER CLASS A4 MALLARD

Length: 21.35 metres
Wheelbase: 18.5 metres
Gauge: 1.44 metres
Weight: 104.6 tonnes
Top speed: 203 kilometres per hour

SMOKESTACK

Mallard had a Kylchap exhaust. Excess steam and smoke from the firebox were mixed to create an even airflow through the fire tubes.

Whistle

Fire tubes

Blastpipe

MALLARD

Smokebox door

Headlight

Buffer

Coupler

Piston

Piston rod

BOILER

This held the water that was heated to make steam. Steam from the cylinders and smoke from the fire tubes collected in the smokebox in front, before leaving through the chimney.

CYLINDERS

Mallard had three cylinders – two on the outside at the front of the locomotive and one on the inside, between them. The cylinders contained pistons, which were pushed out by the steam and this in turn drove the wheels.

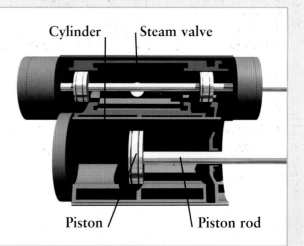

Cylinder   Steam valve

Piston   Piston rod

Driver's cab

Water tank

4468

L N E R

Coal bunker

Tender

Brake shoe

Coupling rods

DRIVE WHEELS

Power from the pistons was transferred through coupling rods to Mallard's six drive wheels. When it was travelling at top speed, the wheels turned 81 times a second.

FIREBOX

Coal was burned to generate the heat needed to turn water to steam. The driver's mate, or fireman, shovelled coal into the firebox from the bunker.

CRAWLER-TRANSPORTER

Built in 1965, NASA's Crawler-Transporters, named Franz and Hans, are the world's biggest self-powered vehicles. Their original job, at the Kennedy Space Center, was to carry the gigantic Saturn V rockets from the assembly buildings to the launch pad. In 1969, the Apollo 11 mission that took the first astronauts to the Moon began its long journey on the top of a Crawler.

DIESEL ENGINE-GENERATORS

The main power for the Crawler comes from four diesel engines. These run generators that provide electricity for the motors, hydraulic pumps, lights and ventilation fans.

HYDRAULIC PUMPS

The Crawler has 12 pumps. These force hydraulic fluid into the pistons that steer it and drive the jacking, equalising and levelling system that keeps the platform level.

Ventilation fans

Corner C   Corner D

PROPULSION TRUCK

Two caterpillar tracks are driven by four electric traction motors. These move the Crawler along the purpose built, 5.6 kilometre crawlerway from the assembly building to the launch pad – a journey that takes about five hours.

Guide tube

Jacking pistons

Steering piston

Engine control room

750 kilowatt engine-generator

Hydraulic oil tank

Access stair (lowered) and walkway

Caterpillar shoes

Drive sprocket

Traction motors

FUEL TANK

The Crawler has two fuel tanks, each holding 19,000 litres of diesel fuel. It uses 3.5 litres of fuel to travel 13 metres.

CRAWLER-TRANSPORTER

Length: 40 metres
Width: 35 metres
Height: 6-8 metres
Top speed: 3.2 kilometres per hour unloaded, 1.6 kilometres per hour loaded
Weight: 2,468 tonnes

Platform

Chassis top

150 kilowatt engine-generator

Second 2,000 kilowatt engine-generator

Corner A

Corner B

WATER RADIATORS

The Crawler needs six radiators to stop its four diesel engines from overheating. 1,900 litres of water are pumped through each radiator.

SPACE SHUTTLE

Since 1981, the Crawlers have been used to carry the Space Shuttle to the launch pad at the Kennedy Space Center. A laser is used to accurately position the Crawler beneath the Mobile Launcher Platform with the Shuttle on top. Hydraulic jacks then raise the Crawler and lift the platform and Shuttle – a total weight of 5,000 tonnes.

External liquid fuel tank

Solid rocket boosters

Space Shuttle

Crawler-Transporter

Mobile launcher platform

OPERATOR'S CAB

The Crawler has two operator's cabs – one on the front and one on the back. To reverse, the driver switches from the cab on corner B to corner D and drives away.

BEDE BD-5J

The Bede BD-5J is the world's smallest jet aeroplane. It was developed in 1973 from the Bede BD-5 – a kit aeroplane that was powered by a rear propeller. The Bede BD-5J is no longer being made. A few are still airworthy however, and the US Department of Defense has certified the design as a manned cruise missile surrogate.

Canopy

COCKPIT

This has room for a single pilot. The large canopy gives great visibility and the seating position is comfortable.

AVIONICS

These are miniaturised, in common with the rest of the plane. The electronics extend to the fuel control system, which is fully automatic.

Instrument panel

UNDERCARRIAGE

The retractable landing gear is built into the fuselage. Although the two back wheels are close together the system is stable.

Air intake

BEDE BD-5J

Wingspan: 5.2 metres
Length: 3.8 metres
Height: 1.6 metres
Top speed: 482 kilometres per hour

FUSELAGE

This is built from aluminium alloy panels coated with foam and fibreglass. The fuselage houses almost all of the plane's essential parts, including the engine.

Engine exhaust pipe

TAIL

The swept-back tail makes the BD-5J look fast. The rudder is built in to the vertical part of the tail.

WINGS

These can be removed, allowing the plane to be towed in a trailer. The wings' shortness and swept-back shape make the BD-5J easy to manoeuvre.

ENGINE

The BD-5J is powered by a French designed and US built Sermel TRS-18-046 turbojet engine. Like the rest of the plane, this engine is unusually small and light, weighing just 30 kilograms – about the same as a nine-year-old child. The engine can produce 148 kilograms of thrust.

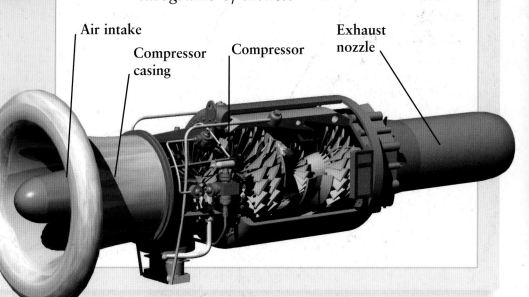

Air intake

Compressor casing

Compressor

Exhaust nozzle

SPIRIT OF AUSTRALIA

Spirit of Australia is the current holder of the water speed record. The jet powered boat set the record at 511.1 kilometres per hour in 1978, on the Blowering Dam reservoir in New South Wales. Spirit of Australia was piloted by Ken Warby. It is now kept at the Australian National Maritime Museum in Sydney.

COCKPIT

This is fully enclosed by a glass canopy which was added after the boat had already tested at 394 km/h.

Fuel tank

Hull

Air intakes

SPONSONS

These extra, miniature hulls are attached to the front of the boat. They give it greater stability when accelerating and help to lift the front off the water at speed.

Low speed

High speed

HYDROPLANES

Spirit of Australia is a hydroplane – a boat designed to travel with almost no contact with the water. Friction from contact with water slows a boat down. At full speed only the rear tip of the hull touches the water's surface.

BODYWORK

Warby designed this to be as aerodynamic as possible. He knew the main factor determining its top speed would be how well it cut through the air.

TAIL

Warby added the tail from a Cessna 172 aeroplane to give added stability.

RIT OF AUSTRALIA
E WORLDS FASTEST BOAT

YS

SE

FOS

Rudder

ENGINE

Spirit of Australia was almost entirely funded by Ken Warby, who spent several years saving up the money to build it. In order to cut costs, he fitted the boat with an old Westinghouse J34 turbojet engine, bought for 65 Australian dollars. Designed in the late 1940s, the Westinghouse J34 was used as the standard engine in several postwar US fighter planes.

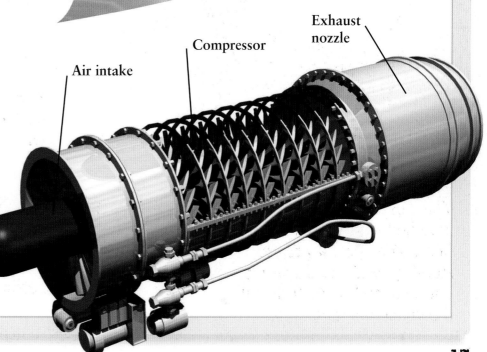

Air intake

Compressor

Exhaust nozzle

THRUST SSC

Thrust SSC is the current holder of the land speed record. SSC stands for SuperSonic Car and Thrust SSC was the first land vehicle to break the sound barrier. When it set the record on 15 October 1997, it reached a staggering 1,228 kilometres per hour. It was exactly 50 years and a day since Chuck Yeager became the first person to break the sound barrier in his Bell X-1 jet aeroplane.

FIRE CONTROL

In such a ground-breaking car the risk of fire is always present. The Thrust SSC has heat sensors in the body of the vehicle and infrared sensors in its cockpit. Extinguishers are fitted around the body of the car.

Fuel tank

COCKPIT

This is near the car's centre of gravity and is entered via the removable canopy. Inside, the instrumentation includes an air speed indicator, converted from a Phantom jet plane's gauge.

Air intake

Nose cone

THRUST SSC

Length: 16.5 metres
Height: 2.1 metres
Width: 3.7 metres
Weight: 10.5 tonnes
Top speed: 1,228 kilometres per hour

Tail

CHASSIS

This is made from welded steel. The body panels are titanium, aluminium and carbon fibre. Although the car is heavy, its weight is not a problem. The engines have the same power as about 800 Ford Focuses.

Parachute

AERODYNAMICS

Thrust SSC has smooth lines, like a jet fighter, to cut through the air. The tail gives downward force to keep it on the ground.

Engine housing

Canopy

ENGINE

Thrust SSC is powered by two Rolls-Royce Spey jet engines. The engines used during the record-breaking run at Black Rock Desert in Nevada were modified slightly by Rolls-Royce engineers to be even more powerful than standard Spey engines.

WHEELS

The car has solid aluminium alloy wheels. When the record was set, each one was rotating at more than 125 times every second.

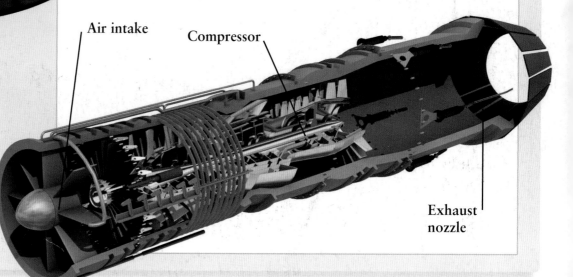

Air intake

Compressor

Exhaust nozzle

X-43A

The X-43A is the world's fastest jet-powered aircraft. In November 2004, it set a new record speed of Mach 9.6, or around 11,265 kilometres per hour, flying at an altitude of 33,528 metres. The X-43A is an unmanned experimental aircraft, designed to send payloads into space.

FUEL

The engine runs on hydrogen fuel. This is ignited with air forced at high speed into the scramjet's air intake.

SILANE TANK

Pyrophoric silane, which ignites on contact with air, is used to start the engine.

HEAT SHIELDS

The nose, tail and wings of the X-43A are covered with a heat resistant, carbon-based material. This protects it from the high temperatures caused by friction as it travels through the air.

Flight management unit

Battery

AERODYNAMICS

The body of the X-43A is shaped to create its own lift, rather than relying on that provided by wings. It is surprisingly stable.

SENSOR UNIT

This detects any changes to the airflow entering the engine's air intake and instructs the linked control system to make the necessary adjustments to compensate. Reliable air flow is vital for scramjet engines.

Scramjet

Rudder

Tail

X-43A
Weight: 999 kilograms
Length: 3.7 metres
Width at widest point: 1.5 metres
Top speed: 11,265 kilometres per hour

Horizontal tail actuators

Nitrogen tank

Water tank

ACTUATOR CONTROL UNIT

This receives instructions from ground crew directing the aircraft's flight and transfers them to the rudder actuator.

RUDDER ACTUATOR

This moves the rudder left or right in response to signals from the actuator control unit.

SCRAMJET

The X-43A is driven by a supersonic combustion ramjet, or scramjet. Like all scramjet engines, this only operates at speeds of Mach 6 or above, so the X-43A requires another engine to carry it to that speed before the scramjet can be started. In its test flights, including the record-breaking flight, it was launched attached to the tip of a Pegasus rocket. This was discarded once the scramjet engine had started to run.

Fuel injection and combustion

Jet exhaust

Air

Air intake

VIRGIN ATLANTIC GLOBALFLYER

The Virgin Atlantic GlobalFlyer holds the record for the fastest non-stop flight around the world without refuelling. Starting on 28 February and finishing on 3 March 2005, the pilot, Steve Fossett, made the journey in 67 hours, 1 minute at an average speed of 590.7 kilometres per hour. The GlobalFlyer was designed by the aerospace engineer Burt Rutan, who had also designed the previous record holder, Voyager.

VIRGIN ATLANTIC GLOBALFLYER

Wingspan: 34.75 metres
Length: 13.44 metres
Height: 4 metres
Top speed: 315 kilometres per hour
Weight (empty): 1,678 kilograms
Weight (full): 10,024 kilograms

WINGS

The wings are built from carbon fibre, making them lightweight but strong. When fully loaded with fuel the wings flexed up to 2.4 metres.

COCKPIT

The cruising height of 13,700 metres meant that the 2.1 metre long cabin had to be pressurised.

FUEL TANKS

There are 13 fuel tanks – one in the main fuselage, two in each boom and four in each wing. Between them they can hold 8,172 kilograms of jet fuel. Before taking the non-stop round-the-world speed record, this plane made the longest ever flight without refuelling – 41,467 kilometres.

Engine cowling

Canopy

Door

Cabin portholes

ENGINE

The GlobalFlyer is powered by a single Williams International FJ44-3 ATW turbofan engine, chosen for its small size and fuel efficiency. It normally uses standard jet fuel, which needs heaters to keep it from freezing at high altitudes. To save the weight of heaters Rutan adjusted the engine to burn JP-3 fuel instead, which has a lower freezing point.

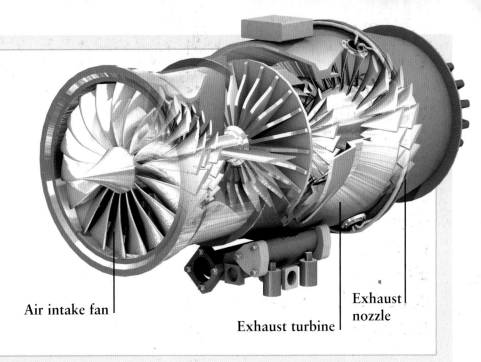

Air intake fan

Exhaust turbine

Exhaust nozzle

PARACHUTES

The GlobalFlyer needed two parachutes to slow it down enough to land. Its ability to glide helped to make it such a fuel-efficient aircraft.

FUSELAGE

The paint on the GlobalFlyer was just 0.06 millimetres thick to help save weight. It was still thick enough to protect the craft from the Sun's heat and radiation.

TAILS

The two tails are small and light, reducing drag and the overall weight of the plane. Their distance from the wing makes the plane more stable

Rudder

Elevator

Tail boom fuel tanks

Wing fuel tanks

UNDERCARRIAGE

The landing gear was lowered using its own weight and raised with compressed air from a paint-ball gun canister.

Ailerons

AIRBUS A380

The Airbus A380 is the world's largest passenger airliner. It made its maiden flight on 27 April 2005, and its first commercial flight on 25 October 2007. Airbus is a European corporation that makes different parts of the plane in different countries. For example, the wings are built in the UK and the tail in Spain.

PASSENGER DECKS

The A380 has two passenger decks, with sections for First Class, Business Class and Economy Class passengers. The number of passengers varies from just over 500 with three classes to more than 850 with only Economy Class.

Internal structure

Stairway

FLIGHT DECK

As on other Airbus planes the A380 uses a 'fly-by-wire' (computer operated) system.

Radar

Baggage containers

AVIONICS

The A380 uses Integrated Modular Avionics, previously used in advanced military aircraft. It has a powerful network systems server that holds all the information and displays it via LCD panels.

BAGGAGE HOLD

Beneath the passenger decks is the baggage hold, where luggage is stored. In future shops, restaurants and other recreational facilities may be housed in this area.

UNDERCARRIAGE

The main undercarriage has 20 wheels, each 1.4 metres in diameter. Two wheels under the aircraft's nose steer the plane.

Outer skin

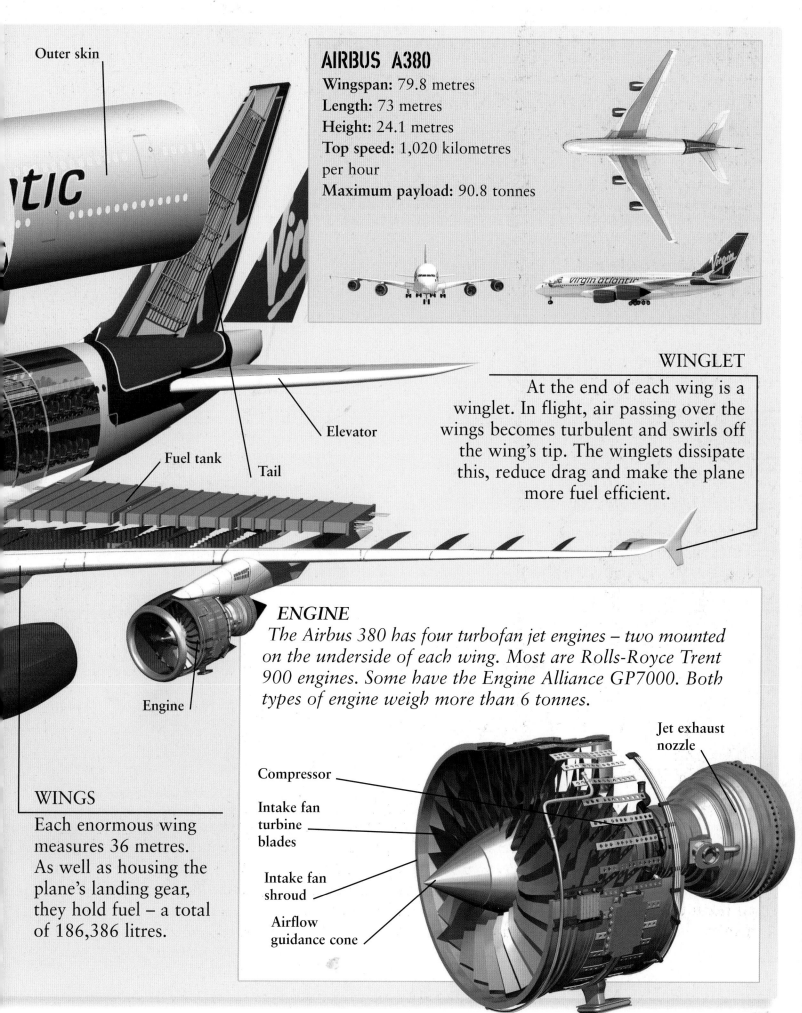

AIRBUS A380

Wingspan: 79.8 metres
Length: 73 metres
Height: 24.1 metres
Top speed: 1,020 kilometres per hour
Maximum payload: 90.8 tonnes

Elevator

Tail

Fuel tank

WINGLET

At the end of each wing is a winglet. In flight, air passing over the wings becomes turbulent and swirls off the wing's tip. The winglets dissipate this, reduce drag and make the plane more fuel efficient.

Engine

ENGINE

The Airbus 380 has four turbofan jet engines – two mounted on the underside of each wing. Most are Rolls-Royce Trent 900 engines. Some have the Engine Alliance GP7000. Both types of engine weigh more than 6 tonnes.

WINGS

Each enormous wing measures 36 metres. As well as housing the plane's landing gear, they hold fuel – a total of 186,386 litres.

Compressor

Intake fan turbine blades

Intake fan shroud

Airflow guidance cone

Jet exhaust nozzle

25

BUGATTI VEYRON

When it was introduced in 2005, the Bugatti Veyron was the world's fastest production road car, capable of reaching 407 kilometres per hour. It accelerates from 0 to 99 kilometres per hour in 2.5 seconds, and takes 24 seconds to reach 322 kilometres per hour from a standing start. A total of 300 are to be built, each costing approximately £1 million.

TAIL WING

When the car reaches 220 kilometres per hour the tail wing automatically lifts into place. Like an upside-down aircraft wing it pushes the rear of the car on to the road, giving the wheels more grip. When the driver brakes, the wing changes its angle and becomes an air brake.

SUSPENSION

At top speed hydraulic motors lower the car's suspension, so it is just 8.9 centimetres above the road.

Gearbox

BUGATTI VEYRON

Length: 4.5 metres
Width: 2 metres
Height: 1.2 metres
Weight: 1.88 tonnes
Top speed: 407 kilometres per hour

BRAKES

The Veyron's brake disks are made from a compound of silicon and carbon – the same material covers the Space Shuttle's nose and is used in bullet proof vests. The brakes bring the Veyron from 400 kilometres per hour to a halt in under 10 seconds.

Fuel tank

WHEELS

The rear tyres are 36.6 centimetres wide and the front tyres 24.1 centimetres. When completely flat they can still run for 201 kilometres at 80 kilometres per hour.

Air scoops

BODYWORK

The driver and passenger are surrounded by an aluminium, steel and carbon frame. This single-piece frame, or monocoque, is designed to protect them in a crash.

INTERIOR

The inside is finished with leather. The dashboard has a large central rev counter surrounded by smaller instruments.

Battery

Headlights

Front gearbox

Driveshaft

RADIATORS

There are 10 radiators on board the Veyron. Eight stop the engine and gearbox from becoming too hot and two keep the driver and passenger cool.

ENGINE

The Veyron has an 8-litre W16 engine – the equivalent of two narrow V8 engines mated side-by-side. Each of the 16 cylinders has four valves, making 64 valves in total. The engine is fed by four turbochargers and has a total output of 1,001 horsepower.

Turbochargers

Exhaust

Rear axle

TGV 4402

TGV 4402 is the fastest train ever to run on conventional rails. On 3 April 2007, it set a new world record speed of 574.8 kilometres per hour. TGV 4402 is a one-off train that was specially modified to make the world record attempt. It is based on the TGV POS, which routinely carries passengers through France at up to 320 kilometres per hour.

TGV 4402

Length: 106 metres
Weight: 268 tonnes
Wheel diameter: 1.092 metres
Top speed: 574.8 kilometres per hour

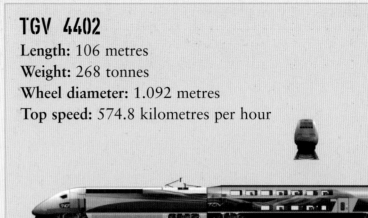

Cooling tanks

DRIVER'S CAB

The cab of TGV 4402 has a comfortable, soft seat for the driver, surrounded by controls.

TRANSFORMERS

These convert the electrical power gathered by the pantograph to a voltage the train's engines can use.

POWER PACK

This receives electricity from the transformers and uses it to drive the wheels of the locomotive.

BRAKES

TGV 4402 has disk brakes on its wheels and dynamic brakes on its axles. Together, these provide enough braking power to stop the train.

PANTOGRAPH

This is used to collect electric current from overhead lines to drive the train. Pantographs are commonly used by trains in France.

TRACK

Unlike the train, LGV Est, where the speed record was achieved, was not modified in any way. It is a standard high-speed train line.

Pneumatic block

Upper deck

Lower deck

DUPLEX CARRIAGES

Three of these double-decker carriages were used between two TGV locomotives to make up the record-breaking train.

MOTOR BOGIE

Each of TGV 4402's two locomotives sits on two of these. For the record attempt two were added to one of the carriages. Despite their name, TGV motor bogies do not have their own motors – instead they use a system of gears to transfer power from the power pack to the wheels.

Permanent-magnet motor

Secondary suspension

Primary suspension

MORE RECORD BREAKERS

Records are constantly broken as advances in technology are made. Electronics and nano-technology (the study of the control of matter on an atomic and molecular scale) are getting tinier and materials for construction are getting lighter and stronger.

The smallest petrol engine can sit on a fingertip and run for two years on a small squirt of lighter fuel – yet the smallest motor ever built was a gold rotor on a nanotube shaft that could ride on the back of a virus! At the other end of the scale engines are built to enormous sizes. The most powerful diesel engine in the world is the Wartsila-Sulzer RTA96-C, designed for large container ships. It stands five stories high, at 13.5 metres, is 27.3 metres long, and weighs over 2,300 tonnes.

CONCORDE
In 1992, a Concorde made the fastest non-orbital circumnavigation, taking 32 hours, 49 minutes and 3 seconds to fly right around the world.

APOLLO 10
Its crew travelled at 39,897 km/h, faster than anyone else in history.

FREEDOM OF THE SEAS
This is the world's largest cruise ship which can carry 3,634 passengers.

BAGGER 288
This is the world's largest tracked vehicle. Unlike NASA's Crawler-Transporter it is powered from an external source.

GLOSSARY

alloy
A mixture of two or more metals, or a metal and another chemical element, such as carbon.

avionics
An abbreviation of 'aviation electronics'. The electical and electronic systems that enable an aircraft or similar vehicle to fly.

carbon fibre
A lightweight but strong material made from microscopic carbon threads.

chassis
The frame that forms the basic skeleton of a motor vehicle. The axles and bodywork are attached to the chassis.

diesel
A type of fuel used by motor vehicles. Diesel is normally oil-based but may also be derived from organic matter.

fuselage
The central body of an aircraft, to which the wings and tail are attached.

hydraulic
Operated by a liquid such as water or oil under high pressure.

infrared
Electromagnetic radiation just beyond the red end of the light spectrum. Infrared radiation is given off by objects warmer than the surrounding air.

locomotive
A self-propelled engine that pushes or pulls a train along tracks. A locomotive may be powered by steam, diesel, or electricity.

NASA
National Aeronautics and Space Administration. The US government agency responsible for the nation's public space programme.

payload
Cargo, such as equipment and satellites, that is carried for a fee.

rudder
A moveable flap used for steering an aeroplane or boat.

supersonic
Faster than the speed of sound (1,235 kilometres per hour).

tender
A wagon designed to carry coal and water for a steam locomotive.

turbofan engine
A jet engine with a fan that blows air on to the burner to provide extra thrust.

undercarriage
The wheels and landing gear of an aircraft.

INDEX